# Sharon Word

# The Word is Alphabet

## "Poems"

Published by:
Intermedia Publishing Group, Inc.
P.O. Box 2825
Peoria, Arizona 85380
www.intermediapub.com

ISBN 978-1-935906-29-2

# Dedication

This alphabet book is dedicated to "all" young children who are excited to learn their ABC's and read. My hope is that the alphabet characters will come alive and motivate them to develop creativity and imagination related to their personal experiences. I also dedicate this book to my children—my son, Rick Bacon, and the memory of my daughter, Jodi Rae Bacon.

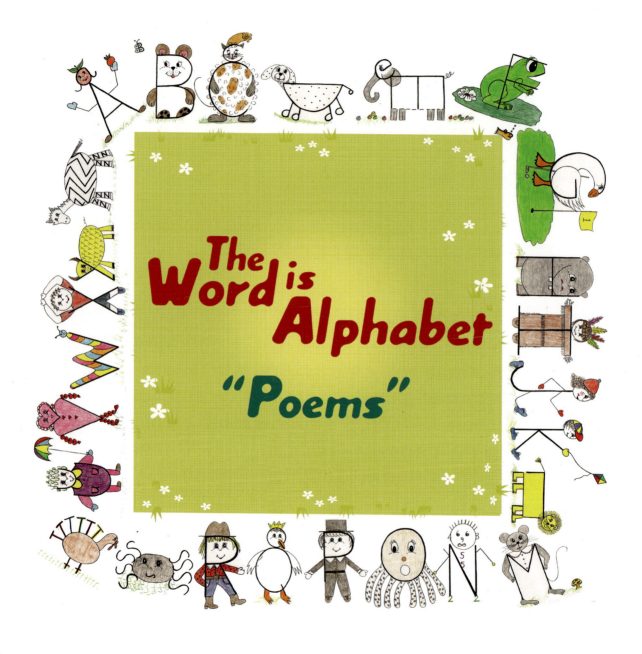

# The Word is Alphabet

## "Poems"

## The Word is "Apple" - Ann Apple

**Ann Apple can be tart or sweet.
She's good to eat for a snack or treat.**

## The Word is "Bear" – Bobbie Bear

**Bobbie Bear gives lots of hugs.**
**Her friends are a bumble bee, a butterfly and a bug.**

# The Word is "Cat" – Curly Cat

**Curly is a cute calico cat.**
**He combs his curls and likes to wear caps.**

## The Word is "Dog" – Dotty Dog

**Dotty Dog is a Dalmatian with many spots.**
**She likes to draw and do dot-to-dots.**

4

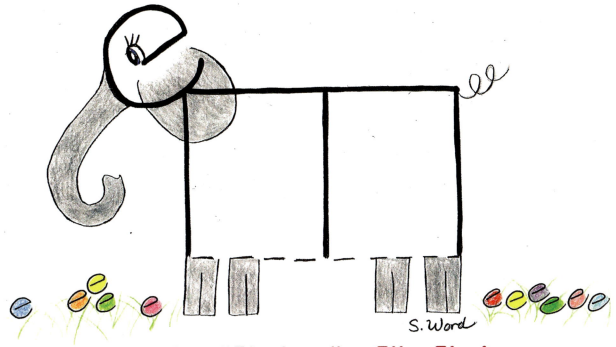

S. Word

## The Word is "Elephant" – Ellie Elephant

**Ellie Elephant eats eleven eggs every day.**
**She is enormous and enjoys exercising each day.**

## The Word is "Frog" – Freddie Frog

**Freddie Frog and his friends have lots of fun.**
**They like to fish and frolic in the sun.**

6

## The Word is "Goose" – Goofy Goose

**Goofy Goose goes golfing every day.
He's getting good and always wants to play.**

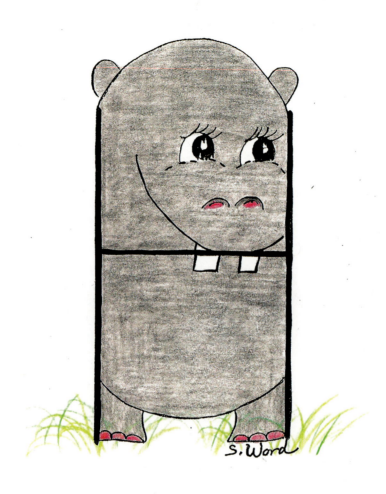

## The Word is "Hippo" – Henry Hippo

**Henry Hippo is heavy, hefty and fat.**
**He hoots and hollers and likes to wear hats.**

## The Word is "Indian" – Ian Indian

Ian Indian lives on the ice.
He inhabits an igloo and it is very nice.

## The Word is "Jogger" – Jodi Jogger

**Jodi Jogger likes to go jogging night and day.
She collects lots of junk along the way.**

## The Word is "Kicker" – Ken Kicker

**Ken Kicker goes to kindergarten and likes school.
He is kind and plays kick ball and knows all the rules.**

## The Word is "Lion" – Leo Lion

Leo Lion laughs a lot and loves to learn.
He does his lessons, listens and always takes turns.

# The Word is "Mouse" – Merry Mouse

**Merry Mouse is a musical mouse.
She marches to music around the house.**

## The Word is "Number" – Number Ned

**Number Ned counts from one to ten.
He needs to practice over and over again.**

S. Word

## *The Word is "Octopus" – Ollie octopus*

**Ollie Octopus lives in the ocean big and deep.
He has eight arms to crawl and creep.**

## The Word is "Pilgrim" – Pilgrim Pete

**Pilgrim Pete has a pink and purple polka dot pig.
They practice the polka and do a jig.**

## The Word is "Queen" – Quiet Queen

**Quiet Queen is a very quaint queen.**
**She makes quilts and they are the nicest you've ever seen.**

## The Word is "Rodeo" – Rodeo Rick

**Rodeo Rick likes to rodeo here and there.
He rides, ropes and races everywhere.**

## The Word is "Spider" - Sally Spider

**Sally Spider likes summer and spring.
She slides, slips, slithers and also likes to swing.**

19

## The Word is "Turkey" – Tommy Turkey

**Tommy Turkey lives under a tall tree.**
**On Tuesdays and Thursdays he watches TV.**

# The Word is "Unusual" – Unusual Ursula

**Unusual Ursula does things upside down.
She plays a ukulele and rides a unicycle all over town.**

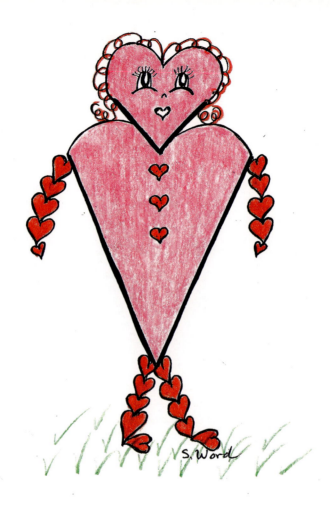

# The Word is "Valentine" – Victoria Valentine

**Victoria Valentine wears a velvet vest.
Her vitamins and vegetables give her lots of zest.**

## The Word is "Worm" – Walter Worm

**Walter Worm wiggles along the way.**
**He likes to waltz every Wednesday.**

# The Word is "Xavier" – Xavier X

**Xavier X does exercises every day.**
**He excels and is excellent in every way.**

## The Word is "Yellow" – Yellow Yak

Yellow Yak does yoga in his yard.
He yells and yodels and is always on guard.

## The Word is "Zebra" – Zelda Zebra

**Zelda Zebra lives in a zoo.**
**Her zip code is 00000 and she knows it too.**

# The Word is "Parents"

The "Word is Alphabet–Poems" is a letter recognitions and phonetics book for young children.  It is related to experiences that children have had or expect to have in their learning endeavors.

Children learn best when they are involved in the learning process. Learning happens by creating experiences in which children are active participants.

This book suggests how to make parents partners in the learning process.  Parents need to be involved in their child's early education through discussion and providing the opportunity for their children to express themselves artistically by using paper, crayons, paint, clay, glue and other familiar materials around the house.

Shopping at the grocery store for food items that relate to the letter can be a learning experience for children. Buy items that start with the letter you are learning.  For example: the Letter A—apples, apricots, asparagus, animal crackers, apple juice or applesauce.  Children will learn to recognize labels, read signs and some may even be motivated to cook.  Let them help you prepare the food for snacks or meals. Cooking can be a new and exciting adventure and again, let your child become involved.

The letters in this book are very easy to draw. Let them draw each character of the alphabet and make their own book.

Parenting can be a challenge, however, it will be the most rewarding endeavor you will ever accomplish in your life. I hope you have fun learning the letters with your child and making the alphabet an exciting and stimulating experience.

# ABC's of Parenting

**This is an alphabet of child raising ideas that may be able to help you through your child's educational journey.**

**A** is for <u>Accountability</u>, <u>Attitude</u> and <u>Acceptance</u>.
Hold your child accountable for their behavior. Attitude is a choice so stay positive. Be accepting and open to new ideas.

**B** is for <u>Boundaries</u>, <u>Behavior</u> and <u>Best</u>.
Set limits and make clear the repercussion of your child's behavior if those limits are exceeded. Do your best at all times.

**C** is for <u>Consequences</u>, <u>Consistency</u> and <u>Consideration</u>.
Consequences need to be enforced for inappropriate behavior. Be firm, fair and consistent and consider all avenues when you discipline.

**D** is for <u>Discipline</u>, <u>Denial</u> and <u>Dignity</u>.
Discipline with love and logic. Don't stay in denial but accept with dignity the outcome of the action.

**E** is for <u>Example</u>, <u>Excellence</u> and <u>Enthusiasm</u>.
Be a good role model and set a good example. Strive for excellence and keep enthusiastic about life.

**F** is for <u>Forgiveness</u>, <u>Fun</u> and <u>Friendships</u>.
Practice and teach the importance of forgiveness. Learning should be fun and make many friends along life's way.

**G** is for <u>Giving</u>, <u>Goals</u> and <u>Good</u>.
It is better to give than receive. Share and joy will come your way. Set short term goals and look for the good in people.

**H** is for <u>Humor</u>, <u>Happiness</u>, and <u>Health</u>.
Laughter is good for the soul. Keep a good sense of humor. Be happy and stay healthy.

**I** is for <u>Imagination</u>, <u>Initiative</u>, and <u>Ideals</u>.
Be creative and don't lose your sense of inner child. Take the initiative to get what you want and set goals and ideals that you want to achieve.

**J** is for <u>Justice</u>, <u>Joy</u>, and <u>Journal</u>.
Always be fair. Seek joy in life and keep a journal.

**K** is for <u>Knowing</u> and <u>Kind</u>.
Know your child's friends and parents. Be kind to everyone.

**L**  is for <u>Listening</u>, <u>Learning</u> and <u>Love</u>.
Listen to your child and teach them how to listen to others. Learn something new every day and love one another.

**M**  is for <u>Morals</u>, <u>Manners</u> and <u>Memories</u>.
Be sure your own standard of morals is sound. Teach your child good manners and create memories. That's all we leave in life.

**N**  is for <u>No</u>, <u>Nice</u> and <u>Never</u>.
It is OK to say no. Use it and mean it. Be nice to your neighbors and friends and never give up.

**O**  is for <u>Opportunity</u>, <u>Obstacles</u> and <u>Outdoors</u>.
Give your child opportunities to do activities they enjoy and support them. Face obstacles in life and conquer them. Plan outdoor activities and teach your child about their environment.

**P**  is for <u>Positive</u>, <u>Progressive</u> and <u>Practical</u>.
Be positive and reduce pressure in your child's life. Be progressive and maintain high standards and stay practical in all situations.

**Q**  is for <u>Questions</u> and <u>Quiet</u>.
Give simple answers to your child's questions and make them feel that no question is wrong. Make time in your day for quiet and stillness.

**R**  is for <u>Responsibility</u>, <u>Respect</u> and <u>Rights</u>.
Teach responsibility and make your child accountable for their choices. Show respect, teach respect and earn respect. With rights comes responsibility. Teach your child to respect the rights of others.

**S** is for <u>Sharing</u> and <u>Source</u> of <u>Strength</u>.
Show and Tell is a good way to share something each day with your child. Also share your beliefs with your child.

**T** is for <u>Togetherness</u>, <u>Time</u> and <u>Tolerance</u>.
Set special, designated times to be together as a family but know when to let go. Be tolerant of one another and accept the differences in others.

**U** is for <u>Unique</u>, <u>Unusual</u> and <u>Understanding</u>.
Understand the uniqueness of your child and accept them for who they are.

**V** is for <u>Voice</u>, <u>Vivacious</u> and <u>Vigor</u>.
The tone of your voice can convey more to a child than the words spoken. Be vivacious and fun and fill your life with vim and vigor.

**W** is for <u>Words—Who, What, Where, When and Why</u>.
Keep your word. Broken promises destroy trust. Answer all the five W's.

**X** is <u>for eXamine</u>, <u>eXcellence</u> and <u>eXercise</u>.
Examine constantly and be aware. Strive for excellence and keep fit and active by exercising every day.

**Y** is for <u>You</u>.
Take care of yourself mentally, emotionally and physically. God created one YOU and just remember YOU are special.

**Z** is for <u>Zest</u>.
Develop a zest for life—it goes quickly so enjoy the ride.

# About the Author

## What's the word? The Word is "Sharon."

Sharon Word holds a Bachelor of Music Education and a Masters Degree in Curriculum and Instruction. She taught for thirty-two years in the Denver Public Schools in Colorado. Sharon won the Denver Teachers' Award for Excellence—Teacher of the Year in 1995. She wrote and created an early childhood- kindergarten curriculum which included poems, stories, music, art, math and science. Sharon is a super, sensational senior. She was born on the fourth of July and is still sparkling, sizzling, booming and exploding her energy and enthusiasm into the universe. She is the "first" word, the "last" word and wants to "spread" the word through her creative writing talents of children's poems, stories, and music. Sharon is retired and lives part time in Denver, Colorado and Sun City, Arizona with her husband, Phill.

**Intermedia Publishing Group**

## Do you need a speaker?

Do you want Sharon Word to speak to your group or event? Then contact Larry Davis at: **(623) 337-8710** or email: **ldavis@intermediapr.com** or use the contact form at: **www.intermediapr.com**.

Whether you want to purchase bulk copies of *The Word is Alphabet* or buy another book for a friend, get it now at: **www.imprbooks.com**.

**If you have a book that you would like to publish**, contact Terry Whalin, Publisher, at Intermedia Publishing Group, (623) 337-8710 or email: twhalin@intermediapub.com or use the contact form at: www.intermediapub.com.